James Edward Talmage

The Book of Mormon

Two Lectures

James Edward Talmage

The Book of Mormon
Two Lectures

ISBN/EAN: 9783337298364

Printed in Europe, USA, Canada, Australia, Japan

Cover: Foto ©Lupo / pixelio.de

More available books at **www.hansebooks.com**

"THE BOOK OF MORMON"

AN ACCOUNT OF ITS ORIGIN, WITH EVIDENCES OF
ITS GENUINENESS AND AUTHENTICITY.

TWO LECTURES

BY

DR. JAMES E. TALMAGE.

PREPARED BY APPOINTMENT; AND PUBLISHED BY THE
CHURCH OF JESUS CHRIST OF LATTER-DAY SAINTS.

THE DESERET NEWS,
SALT LAKE CITY, UTAH,
1899.

PREFATORY.

The matter presented in the following pages is published as Lectures XIV and XV, in the series entitled "The Articles of Faith," dealing with the principal doctrines of the Church of Jesus Christ of Latter-day Saints, prepared and delivered by Dr. James E. Talmage, and published by the Church, 1899. The two Lectures are presented in this separate form for the use and benefit of investigators and students, who desire to learn something of the most noted and characteristic volume among the Standard Works of the Church.

Article 8:—"We believe the Bible to be the
word of God, as far as it is translated correctly;
we also believe the Book of Mormon to be the
word of God."

"THE BOOK OF MORMON."

LECTURE I.

DESCRIPTION AND ORIGIN.

1. **What is the Book of Mormon?**—The claims made for the Book of Mormon affirm it to be a divinely inspired record, made by the prophets of the ancient peoples who inhabited the American continent for centuries before and immediately after the time of Christ; which record has been translated in the present generation through the gift of God and by His special appointment. The authorized and inspired translator of these sacred scriptures, through whose instrumentality they have been given to the world in modern language, is Joseph Smith, whose first acquaintance with the plates was mentioned in a preceding lecture.[a] As stated, on the 21st of September, 1823, Joseph Smith received, in answer to fervent prayer, a visitation from an angelic personage, who gave his name as Moroni; subsequent revelations showed him to be the last of a long line of prophets whose translated writings constitute the Book of Mormon; by him the ancient records had been closed; by him the graven plates had been deposited in the earth; and through his ministration they were brought into the possession of the modern prophet and seer whose work of translation is now before us.

2. On the occasion of Moroni's first visit to Joseph Smith, the angelic visitor declared the existence of the record, which, he said, was engraved on plates of gold,

---

[a] See No. 1 of the Lectures on "The Articles of Faith:" published by the Church, Salt Lake City, 1899.

at that time lying buried in the side of a hill near Joseph's home. The hill, which was known by one division of the ancient peoples as Cumorah, by another as Ramah, is situated near Palmyra in the county of Wayne, State of New York. The precise spot where the plates lay was shown to Joseph in vision; and he had no difficulty in finding it on the day following the visitation referred to. Joseph's statement of Moroni's declaration concerning the plates is as follows:—"He said there was a book deposited, written upon gold plates, giving an account of the former inhabitants of this continent, and the source from which they sprang. He also said that the fulness of the everlasting gospel was contained in it, as delivered by the Savior to the ancient inhabitants. Also, that there were two stones in silver bows, (and these stones, fastened to a breast-plate, constituted what is called the Urim and Thummim), deposited with the plates; and the possession and use of these stones was what constituted Seers in ancient or former times; and that God had prepared them for the purpose of translating the book."[b]

3. Joseph found a large stone at the indicated spot on the hill Cumorah; beneath the stone was a box, also of stone; the lid of this he raised by means of a lever; then he saw within the box the plates, and the breastplate with the Urim and Thummim, as described by the angel. As he was about to remove the contents of the box, Moroni again appeared before him, and forbade him taking the sacred things at that time, saying that four years must pass before they would be committed to his personal care; and that in the meantime, Joseph would be required to visit the place at yearly intervals; this the youthful revelator did, receiving on each occasion additional instruction concerning the record and God's purposes with it. On the 22nd of Septem-

b Pearl of Great Price, p. 94 (1888 ed.)

ber, 1827, Joseph received from the angel Moroni, the plates, and the Urim and Thummim with the breastplate. He was instructed to guard them with strict care, and was promised that if he used his best efforts to protect them, they would be preserved inviolate in his hands; and that on the completion of the labor of translation, Moroni would visit him again, and receive the plates.

4. The reason prompting the angelic caution regarding Joseph's care of the treasures soon appeared; thrice in the course of his brief journey homeward with the sacred relics, he was attacked; but by Divine aid he was enabled to withstand his assailants; and finally reached his home with the plates and other articles unharmed. These attacks were but the beginning of a siege of persecution which was relentlessly waged against him by the powers of evil as long as the plates remained in his custody. News that he had the golden record in his possession soon spread; and numerous attempts, many of them violent, were made to wrest the plates from his hands. But they were preserved; and, slowly, with many hindrances incident to persecution by the wicked, and to the conditions of his own poverty which made it necessary for him to toil and left little leisure for the appointed labor, Joseph proceeded with the translation; and in 1830, the Book of Mormon was first published to the world.

5. The Title Page of the Book of Mormon:—Our best answer to the question: What is the Book of Mormon? is found on the title page to the volume. Thereon we read:

"The Book of Mormon: an account written by the hand of Mormon, upon plates taken from the plates of Nephi. Wherefore it is an abridgment of the record of the people of Nephi, and also of the Lamanites; written to the Lamanites who are a remnant of the house of Israel; and also to Jew and Gentile: written by way of commandment, and also by the spirit of prophecy and of revelation. Written and sealed up, and hid up unto the Lord, that they might not be destroyed; to come forth by the gift and power of God unto the interpretation thereof: sealed by the hand of Moroni, and hid up unto the Lord, to come forth in due time by the way of Gentile; the interpretation thereof by the gift of God.

"An abridgment taken from the Book of Ether also; which is a record of the people of Jared; who were scattered at the time the Lord confounded the language of the people when they were building a tower to get to heaven; which is to show unto the remnant of the House of Israel what great things the Lord hath done for their fathers; and that they may know the covenants of the Lord, that they are not cast off forever; and also to the convincing of the Jew and Gentile that Jesus is the Christ, the Eternal God, manifesting Himself unto all nations. And now, if there are faults, they are the mistakes of men: wherefore condemn not the things of God, that ye may be found spotless at the judgment seat of Christ."

This combined title and preface is a translation from the last page of the plates, and was presumably written by Moroni, who, as before stated, sealed and hid up the book in former days.[c]

6. **Main Divisions of the Book:**—From the title page, we learn that in the Book of Mormon we have to deal with the histories of two great nations, who flourished in America as the descendants of small colonies brought hither from the eastern continent by Divine direction. Of these we may conveniently speak as the Nephites and the Jaredites.

7. **The Nephite Nation** was the later, and in point of the fulness of the records, the more important. The progenitors of this nation were led from Jerusalem 600 B. C., by Lehi, a Jewish prophet of the tribe of Manasseh. His immediate family, at the time of their departure from Jerusalem, comprised his wife Sariah, and their sons Laman,

---

c See note 1, p. 22.

Lemuel, Sam, and Nephi; at a later stage of the history, daughters are mentioned, but whether any of these were born before the family exodus we are not told. Beside his own family, the colony of Lehi included Zoram, and Ishmael, the latter an Israelite of the tribe of Ephraim. Ishmael, with his family, joined Lehi in the wilderness; and his descendants were numbered with the nation of whom we are speaking. The company journeyed somewhat east of south, keeping near the borders of the Red Sea; then, changing their course to the eastward, crossed the peninsula of Arabia; and there on the shores of the Arabian Sea, built and provisioned a vessel in which they committed themselves to Divine care upon the waters. Their voyage carried them eastward across the Indian Ocean, then over the south Pacific Ocean to the western coast of South America, whereon they landed (590 B. C.) probably somewhere near the site of the present city of Valparaiso in Chile.

8. The people established themselves on what to them was the land of promise; many children were born, and in the course of a few generations a numerous posterity held possession of the land. After the death of Lehi, a division occurred, some of the people accepting as their leader, Nephi, who had been duly appointed to the prophetic office; while the rest proclaimed Laman, the eldest of Lehi's sons, as their chief. Henceforth the divided people were known as Nephites and Lamanites respectively. At times they observed toward each other fairly friendly relations; but generally they were opposed, the Lamanites manifesting implacable hatred and hostility toward their Nephite kindred. The Nephites advanced in the arts of civilization, built large cities, and established prosperous commonwealths; yet they often fell into transgression; and the Lord chastened them by making their foes victorious. They

spread northward, occupying the northern part of South America; then, crossing the Isthmus, they extended their domain over the southern, central, and eastern portions of what is now the United States of America. The Lamanites, while increasing in numbers, fell under the curse of darkness; they became dark in skin and benighted in spirit, forgot the God of their fathers, lived a wild nomadic life, and degenerated into the fallen state in which the American Indians,—their lineal descendants,—were found by those who re-discovered the western continent in later times.

9. The final struggles between Nephites and Lamanites were waged in the vicinity of the hill Cumorah, in what is now the state of New York, resulting in the entire destruction of the Nephites, about 400 A. D. The last Nephite representative was Moroni, who, wandering for safety from place to place, daily expecting death from the victorious Lamanites who had decreed the absolute extinction of their white kindred, wrote the concluding parts of the Book of Mormon, hid the record in Cumorah, and soon there-after died. It was this same Moroni, who, as a resurrected being, gave the records into the hands of Joseph Smith in the present dispensation.

10. **The Jaredite Nation:**—Of the two nations whose histories constitute the Book of Mormon, the first in order of time consisted of the people of Jared, who followed their leader from the Tower of Babel at the time of the confusion of tongues. Their history was written on twenty-four plates of gold, by Ether the last of their prophets, who, fore-seeing the destruction of his people because of their wickedness, hid away the historical plates. They were afterward found, B. C. 123, by an expedition sent out by King Limhi, a Nephite ruler. The record engraved on these plates was subsequently abridged by Moroni, and the condensed account was attached by him to the Book of

Mormon record; it appears in the modern translation under the name of the Book of Ether.

11. The first and chief prophet of the Jaredites is not mentioned by name in the record as we have it; he is known only as the brother of Jared. Of the people, we learn that amid the confusion of Babel, Jared and his brother importuned the Lord that He would spare them and their associates from the impending disruption. Their prayer was heard, and the Lord led them with a considerable company, who, like themselves, were free from the taint of idolatry, away from their homes, promising to conduct them to a land choice above all other lands. Their course of travel is not given with exactness; we learn only that they reached the ocean, and there constructed eight vessels, called barges, in which they set out upon the waters. These vessels were small and dark within; but the Lord made luminous certain stones, which gave light to the imprisoned voyagers. After a passage of three hundred and forty-four days, the colony landed on the western shore of North America, probably at a place south of the Gulf of California, and north of the Isthmus of Panama.

12. Here they became a flourishing nation; but, giving way in time to internal dissensions, they divided into factions, which warred with one another until the people were totally destroyed. This destruction, which occurred near the hill Ramah, afterward known among the Nephites as Cumorah, probably took place at about the time of Lehi's landing in South America,—590 B.C. The last representative of the ill-fated race was Coriantumr, the former king, concerning whom Ether had prophesied that he should survive all his subjects, and live to see another people in possession of the land. This prediction was fulfilled in that the king, whose people had become extinct, came, in the course of his solitary wanderings, to a region occupied by

the people of Mulek, who are to be mentioned here as the third ancient colony of emigrants from the eastern continent.

13. *Mulek*, we are told, was the son of Zedekiah king of Judah, an infant at the time of his brothers' violent deaths and his father's cruel torture at the hands of the king of Babylon.[d] Eleven years after Lehi's departure from Jerusalem, another colony was led from the city, amongst whom was Mulek. His name has been given to the people, probably on account of his recognized rights of leadership by virtue of his lineage. The Book of Mormon record concerning Mulek and his people is scanty; we learn, however, that the colony was brought across the waters, to a landing on the northern part of the continent. The descendants of this colony were discovered by the Nephites under Mosiah; they had grown numerous, but, having had no scriptures for their guidance, had fallen into a condition of spiritual darkness. They joined the Nephites, and their history is merged into that of the greater nation.[e] The Nephites gave to North America the name, Land of Mulek.

THE ANCIENT PLATES AND THE MODERN TRANSLATION.

14. **The Plates of the Book of Mormon** as delivered by the angel Moroni to Joseph Smith, according to the description given by the modern prophet, were of gold, of uniform size, each about seven inches wide by eight inches long; in thickness, a little less than ordinary sheet tin; they were fastened together by three rings running through the plates near one edge; together they formed a book nearly six inches in thickness, but not all has been translated, a part being sealed. Both sides of the plates were engraved with small and beautiful characters, described by those who ex-

---

d See II Kings xxv. 7.
e Omni i. 12-19.

amined them as of curious workmanship, with the appearance of ancient origin.

15. Three classes of plates are mentioned on the title page of the Book of Mormon, viz:—

(1.) *The Plates of Nephi;* which, as will be shown, were of two kinds:—(a) the larger plates; (b) the smaller plates.

(2.) *The Plates of Mormon*, containing an abridgment from the plates of Nephi, with additions made by Mormon and his son Moroni.

(3.) *The Plates of Ether*, containing as we have seen, the history of the Jaredites.

To these may be added another set of plates, as being mentioned in the Book of Mormon, viz:

(4.) *The Brass Plates of Laban*, brought by Lehi's people from Jerusalem, and containing Jewish scriptures and genealogies; many extracts from which appear in the Nephite records. We have now to consider more particularly the plates of Nephi, and Mormon's abridgment thereof.

16. **The Plates of Nephi** are so named from the fact that they were prepared, and their record was begun, by Nephi, the son of Lehi. These plates were of two kinds,*f* which may be distinguished as the "larger plates," and the "smaller plates." Nephi began his labors as a recorder by engraving on plates of gold a historical account of his people, from the time his father left Jerusalem. This account recited the story of their wanderings, their prosperity, and their distress, the reigns of their kings, and the wars and contentions of the people; the record was in the nature of a secular history. These plates were handed from one recorder to another throughout the generations of the Nephite people; so that at the time they were abridged by Mormon, the record covered a period of about a thousand years, dating from 600 B. C., the time of Lehi's

f I Nephi ix; xix, 1-5; II Nephi v, 30; Jacob i, 1-4; Words of Mormon i, 3-7.

exodus from Jerusalem. Although these plates bore the name of their maker, who was also the first of the writers, the separate work of each recorder is known in general by his specific name, so that the record is made up of many distinct books.

17. By command of the Lord, Nephi made other plates, upon which he recorded particularly the ecclesiastical history of his people, citing only such instances of other events as seemed necessary to the proper sequence of the narrative. "I have received a commandment of the Lord," says Nephi, "that I should make these plates for the special purpose that there should be an account engraven of the ministry of my people."[g] The object of this double line of history was unknown to Nephi, it was enough for him that the Lord required the labor; that it was for a wise purpose will be shown.

18. **Mormon's Abridgment:**—In the course of time, the records that had accumulated as the history of the people grew, fell into the hands of Mormon,[h] and he undertook to make an abridgment of these extensive works, upon plates made with his own hands.[i] By such a course, a record was prepared more concise and more nearly uniform in style, language, and treatment, than could possibly be the case with the varied writings of so many authors as had contributed to the great history during the thousand years of its growth. Mormon recognizes and testifies to the inspiration of God by which he was moved to undertake the great labor.[j] In preparing this shorter history, Mormon preserved the same division of the record into books according to the arrangement of the originals; and thus, though the language may be that of Mormon, except in cases of quotations

---

g 1 Nephi ix, 3.
h Words of Mormon i, 11; Mormon i, 1-4; iv, 23.
i III Nephi v, 8-11.
j III Nephi v, 14-19.

from the plates of Nephi, which are indeed numerous, we find the Books of Nephi, the Book of Alma, the Book of Helaman, etc., the form of speech known as the first person being generally preserved.

19. When Mormon, in the course of his abridgment, had reached the time of King Benjamin's reign, he was deeply impressed with the record engraved on the smaller plates of Nephi,—the history of God's dealings with the people during the period of about four centuries, extending from the time of Lehi's exodus from Jerusalem down to the time of King Benjamin. This record, comprising so much of prophecy concerning the mission of the Savior, was regarded by Mormon with more than ordinary favor. Of these plates he attempted no transcript, but included the originals with his own abridgment of the larger plates, making of the two one book. The record as compiled by Mormon, contained, therefore, a double account of the descendants of Lehi for the first four hundred years of their history,—the brief secular history condensed from the larger plates, and the full text on the smaller plates. In solemn language, and with an emphasis which subsequent events have shown to be significant, Mormon declares the hidden wisdom of the Divine purpose in this duplication:—"And I do this for a wise purpose; for thus it whispereth me, according to the workings of the Spirit of the Lord which is in me. And now, I do not know all things; but the Lord knoweth all things which are to come; wherefore, he worketh in me to do according to his will."[k]

20. **The Lord's Purpose** in the matter of preparing and of preserving the smaller plates as testified of by Mormon, and also by Nephi,[l] is rendered plain from certain circumstances in this dispensation attending the translation of the rec-

---

k Words of Mormon i, 7.
l I Nephi ix, 5.

ords by Joseph Smith. When the prophet had prepared a translation of the first part of the writings of Mormon, the manuscript was won from his care through the unrighteous solicitations of Martin Harris, to whom he considered himself in a degree indebted for fianancial assistance in the work of publication. This manuscript, in all 116 pages, was never returned to Joseph, but, through the dark schemes of evil powers, it fell into the hands of enemies, who straightway laid a wicked plan to ridicule the translator, and thwart the purposes of God. This evil design was that they wait until Joseph had re-translated the missing matter, when the stolen manuscript, which in the meantime had been altered so that the words were made to express the contrary from the true record, would be set forth as a proof that the prophet was unable to translate the same passages twice alike. But the Lord's wisdom interposed to bring to naught these dark designs.

21. Having chastened the Prophet by depriving him for a season of his gift to translate, as also of the custody of the sacred records, and this for his dereliction in permitting the writings to pass into unappointed hands, the Lord graciously restored His penitent servant to favor, and revealed to him the designs of his enemies;[m] at the same time showing how these evil machinations should be made to fail. Joseph was instructed, therefore, not to attempt a re-translation of that part of Mormon's abridgment, the first translation of which had been stolen; but instead, to translate the record of the same events from the plates of Nephi,—the set of smaller plates which Mormon had incorporated with his own writings. The translation so made was therefore published as the record of Nephi, and not as the writing of Mormon; and thus no second translation was made of the parts from which the stolen manuscript had been prepared.

---

m Doctrine and Covenants, x.

22. **The Translation of the Book of Mormon** was effected through the power of God manifested in the bestowal of the gift of revelation. The book professes not to be dependent upon the wisdom or learning of man; its translator was not versed in linguistics; his qualifications were of a different and of a far more efficient order. With the plates, Joseph Smith received from the angel other sacred treasures, including a breastplate, to which were attached the Urim and Thummim,[n] called by the Nephites, *Interpreters*; and by the use of these he was enabled to render the ancient records in our modern tongue. The details of the work of translation have not been recorded, beyond the statement that the translator examined the engraved characters by means of the sacred instruments, and then dictated to the scribe the English sentences.

23. Joseph began his work with the plates by patiently copying a number of characters, adding to some of the pages thus prepared, the translations. The prophet's first assistant in the labor, Martin Harris, obtained permission to take away some of these transcripts, with the purpose of submitting them to the examination of men learned in ancient languages. He placed some of the sheets before Professor Charles Anthon, of Columbia College, who, after careful examination, certified that the characters were in general of the ancient Egyptian order, and that the accompanying translations appeared to be correct. Hearing how this ancient record came into Joseph's hands, Professor Anthon requested Mr. Harris to bring the original book for examination, stating that he would undertake the translation of the entire work; then, learning that a part of the book was sealed, he remarked, "I cannot read a sealed book;" and thus unwittingly did this man fulfil the prophecy of Isaiah concerning the coming forth of the volume:—"And the vision of all

n Doc. and Cov. x, 1; xvii, 1; cxxx, 8, 9; Mos. viii, 13-19; Ether iii, 23-28.

2

is become unto you as the words of a book that is sealed, which men deliver to one that is learned, saying, read this, I pray thee, and he saith, I cannot, for it is sealed."[a] Another linguist, a Dr. Mitchell, of New York, having examined the characters, gave concerning them a testimony in all important respects corresponding to that of Prof. Anthon.

24.   **Arrangement of the Book of Mormon:**—The Book of Mormon comprises fifteen separate parts, commonly called books, distinguished by the names of their principal authors. Of these, the first six books, viz., I and II Nephi, Jacob, Enos, Jarom, and Omni, are literal translations from corresponding portions of the smaller plates of Nephi. The body of the volume, from the Book of Mosiah to Mormon, chapter vii, inclusive, is the translation of Mormon's abridgment of the larger plates of Nephi. Between the books of Jarom and Mosiah, "The Words of Mormon" occur, connecting the record of Nephi as engraved on the smaller plates, with Mormon's abridgment of the larger plates for the periods following. The Words of Mormon may be regarded as a brief explanation of the preceding portions of the work, and an announcement of the parts then to follow. The last part of the Book of Mormon, from the beginning of Mormon viii, to the end of the volume, is in the language of Moroni, the son of Mormon, who first proceeds to finish the record of his father, and then adds an abridgment of a set of plates which contained an account of the Jaredites; this appears as the Book of Ether.

25.   At the time of Moroni's writing, he stood alone,—the sole surviving representative of his people. The last of the terrible wars between Nephites and Lamanites had resulted in the annihilation of the former as a people; and Moroni supposed that his abridgment of the Book of Ether would be his last literary work; but, finding himself mirac-

---

a Isaiah xxix, 11

ulously preserved at the conclusion of that undertaking, he added the parts known to us as the Book of Moroni, containing accounts of the ceremonies of ordination, baptism, administration of the sacrament, etc., and a record of certain utterances and writings of his father Mormon.

THE GENUINENESS OF THE BOOK OF MORMON.

26. The earnest student of the Book of Mormon will be most concerned in his consideration of the reliability of the great record; and this subject may be conveniently considered under two headings: 1st, the genuineness and integrity of the Book of Mormon, i. e., the evidence that the book is what it professes to be,—an actual translation of ancient records; 2nd, the authenticity of the original writings, as shown by internal and external evidence.

27. **The Genuineness of the Book** will appear to anyone who undertakes an impartial investigation into the circumstances attending its coming forth. The many so-called theories of its origin, advanced by prejudiced opponents to the work of God, are in general too inconsistent, and in most instances too thoroughly puerile, to merit serious consideration. Such fancies as are set forth in representations of the Book of Mormon as the production of a single author or of men working in collusion, as a work of fiction, or in any manner as a modern composition, are their own refutation.[o] The sacred character of the plates forbade their display as a means of gratifying personal curiosity; nevertheless a number of reputable witnesses examined them, and these men have given to the world their solemn testimony of the fact. In June, 1829, the prophecies respecting the witnesses by whose testimony the word of God as set forth in the Book of Mormon was to be established,[p] saw its

o See Note 2.

p II Nephi xi, 3; xxvii, 12-13; Ether v, 3-4; see also Doc. and Cov. v, 11-15; xvii, 1-9.

fulfilment in a manifestation of Divine power, demonstrating the genuineness of the record to three men, whose affirmations accompany all editions of the book.

28. **The Testimony of Three Witnesses:**—Be it known unto all nations, kindreds, tongues, and people unto whom this work shall come, that we, through the grace of God the Father, and our Lord Jesus Christ, have seen the plates which contain this record, which is a record of the people of Nephi, and also of the Lamanites, their brethren, and also of the people of Jared, who came from the tower of which hath been spoken; and we also know that they have been translated by the gift and power of God, for his voice hath declared it unto us,[q] wherefore we know of a surety that the work is true. And we also testify that we have seen the engravings[r] which are upon the plates; and they have been shown unto us by the power of God, and not of man. And we declare with words of soberness, that an angel of God came down from heaven,[s] and he brought and laid before our eyes, that we beheld and saw the plates, and the engravings thereon; and we know that it is by the grace of God the Father, and our Lord Jesus Christ, that we beheld and bear record that these things are true; and it is marvelous in our eyes, nevertheless the voice of the Lord commanded us that we should bear record of it; wherefore, to be obedient unto the commandments of God, we bear testimony of these things. And we know that if we are faithful in Christ, we shall rid our garments of the blood of all men, and be found spotless before the judgment-seat of Christ, and shall dwell with him eternally in the heavens. And the honor be to the Father, and to the Son, and to the Holy Ghost, which is one God. Amen.

OLIVER COWDERY,
DAVID WHITMER,
MARTIN HARRIS.

29. The testimony so declared was never revoked, or even modified by any one of the witnesses whose names are sub-

---

q Doc. and Cov. xvii, 6; xx, 8.

r II Nephi v, 32; Alma lxiii, 12; Mormon i, 3.

s See History of Joseph Smith, June, 1829.

scribed to the foregoing,' though all of them withdrew from the Church, and indulged in feelings amounting almost to hatred toward Joseph Smith. To the last of their lives, they maintained the same solemn declaration of the angelic visit, and the testimony that had been implanted in their hearts. Shortly after the witnessing of the plates by the three, other eight persons were permitted to see and handle the ancient records; and in this also was prophecy fulfilled, in that it was of old declared, that beside the three, "God sendeth more witnesses,"" whose testimony shall be added to that of the three. It was presumably in July, 1829, that Joseph Smith showed the plates to the eight whose names are attached to the following certificate.

30. **The Testimony of Eight Witnesses:**—Be it known unto all nations, kindreds, tongues, and people unto whom this work shall come, that Joseph Smith, Jun., the translator of this work, has shown unto us the plates of which hath been spoken, which have the appearance of gold; and as many of the leaves as the said Smith has translated, we did handle with our hands; and we also saw the engravings thereon, all of which has the appearance of ancient work, and of curious workmanship. And this we bear record with words of soberness, that the said Smith has shown unto us, for we have seen and hefted, and know of a surety that the said Smith has got the plates of which we have spoken. And we give our names unto the world, to witness unto the world that which we have seen; and we lie not, God bearing witness of it.

CHRISTIAN WHITMER,
JACOB WHITMER,
PETER WHITMER, JUN.,
JOHN WHITMER,
HIRAM PAGE,
JOSEPH SMITH, SEN.,
HYRUM SMITH,
SAMUEL H. SMITH.

31. Three of the eight witnesses died out of the Church, yet not one of the whole number ever was known to deny

t See Note 3.
u II Nephi xi, 3

his testimony concerning the Book of Mormon." Here then are proofs of varied kinds regarding the reliability of this volume. Learned linguists pronounce the characters genuine; eleven men of honest report make solemn oath of the appearance of the plates; and the nature of the book itself sustains the claim that it is nothing more nor less than a translation of ancient records.

NOTES.

1. **Book of Mormon Title Page:**—"I wish to mention here that the title page of the Book of Mormon is a literal translation, taken from the very last leaf on the left hand side of the collection or book of plates, which contained the record which has been translated, the language of the whole running the same as all Hebrew writing in general; and that said title page is not by any means a modern composition, either of mine or any other man who has lived or does live in this generation."—*Joseph Smith.*

2. **Theories concerning the Origin of the Book of Mormon: The Spaulding Story:**—The true account of the origin of the Book of Mormon was rejected by the public in general, who thus assumed the responsibility of explaining in some plausible way the source of the record. Many vague theories, based on the incredible assumption that the book was the work of a single author, were put forward; of these, the most famous, and, indeed, the only one that lived long enough in public favor to be discussed, is the so-called "Spaulding Story." Solomon Spaulding, a clergyman of Amity, Pa., wrote a romance, to which no title other than "Manuscript Story" was prefixed. Twenty years after the author's death, one Hurlburt, an apostate from the Church of Jesus Christ of Latter-day Saints, announced a resemblance between the story and the Book of Mormon, and expressed his conviction that the work presented to the world by Joseph Smith was nothing but Spaulding's romance revised and amplified. The manuscript was lost for a time, and, in the absence of proof to the contrary, stories of the parallelism between the two works multiplied. But, by a fortunate circumstance, in 1884, President James H. Fairchild of Oberlin College, Ohio, and a literary friend, one Mr. Rice, in examining a heterogeneous collection of old papers that had been purchased by Mr. Rice, found the original story. The gentlemen made a careful comparison of the manuscript and the Book of Mormon; and, with the sole desire of subserving the purposes of truth, made public their results. Pres. Fairchild published an article in the *New York Observer*, Feb. 5, 1885, in which he said:—"The theory of the origin of the Book of Mormon in the traditional manuscript of Solomon Spaulding will probably have to be relinquished. * * * Mr. Rice, myself and others compared it [the Spaulding manuscript] with the Book of Mormon and could detect no resemblance between the two. * * * Some other explanation of the Book of Mormon must be found, if any explanation is required."

---

v See Note 4.

The manuscript was deposited in the library of Oberlin College where it now reposes. Still, the theory of the "Manuscript Found," as Spaulding's story has come to be known, is occasionally pressed into service in the cause of anti-"Mormon" zeal, by some whom we will charitably believe to be ignorant of the facts set forth by Pres. Fairchild. A letter of more recent date, written by that honorable gentleman in reply to an enquiring correspondent, was published in the *Millennial Star*, Liverpool, Nov. 3, 1898, and is as follows:

OBERLIN COLLEGE, OHIO,
October 17, 1895.

J. R. Hindley, Esq.,

DEAR SIR:—We have in our College Library an original manuscript of Solomon Spaulding—unquestionably genuine.

I found it in 1884 in the hands of Hon. L. L. Rice of Honolulu, Hawaiian Islands. He was formerly State Printer at Columbus, O., and before that, publisher of a paper in Painesville, whose preceding publisher had visited Mrs. Spaulding and obtained the manuscript from her. It had lain among his old papers forty years or more, and was brought out by my asking him to look up anti-slavery documents among his papers.

The manuscript has upon it the signatures of several men of Conneaut, O., who had heard Spaulding read it and knew it to be his. No one can see it and question its genuineness. The manuscript has been printed twice at least—once by the Mormons of Salt Lake City, and once by the Josephite Mormons of Iowa. The Utah Mormons obtained the copy of Mr. Rice at Honolulu, and the Josephites got it of me after it came into my possession.

This manuscript is not the original of the Book of Mormon.

Yours very truly,

JAS. H. FAIRCHILD.

Printed copies of the "Manuscript Found" are obtainable, and any enquirer may examine for himself. For further information see "*The Myth of the Manuscript Found*" by Elder George Reynolds, Salt Lake City; Whitney's *History of Utah*, Vol. I, pp. 46-56; Elder George Reynolds' preface to the story as issued by the Deseret News Company, Salt Lake City, 1886; and the story itself.

3. The Three Witnesses:—Oliver Cowdery;—Born at Wells, Rutland Co., Vermont, October, 1805; baptized May 15, 1829; died at Richmond, Mo., March 3, 1850.

David Whitmer:—Born near Harrisburg, Pa., January 7, 1805; baptized June, 1829; excommunicated from the Church, April 13, 1838; died at Richmond, Mo., January 25, 1888.

Martin Harris:—Born at East-town, Saratoga Co., New York, May 18, 1783; baptized 1830; removed to Utah, August, 1870, and died at Clarkston, Cache Co., Utah, July 10, 1875.

4. The Eight Witnesses:—Christian Whitmer:—Born January 18, 1798; baptized April 11, 1830; died in full fellowship in the Church, Clay County, Missouri, November 27, 1835. He was the eldest son of Peter Whitmer.

Jacob Whitmer:—Second son of Peter Whitmer; born in Pennsylvania, January 27, 1800; baptized April 11, 1830; died April 21, 1856, having previously withdrawn from the Church.

Peter Whitmer, Jr.:—Born September 27, 1809; fifth son of Peter Whitmer; baptized June, 1829; died a faithful member of the Church, at or near Liberty, Clay Co., Missouri, September 22, 1836.

John Whitmer:—Third son of Peter Whitmer; born August 27, 1802; baptized June, 1829; excommunicated from the Church March 10, 1838; died at Far West, Missouri, July 11, 1878.

Hiram Page:—Born in Vermont, 1800; baptized April 11, 1830; withdrew from the Church, 1838; died in Ray Co., Missouri, August 12, 1852.

Joseph Smith, Sen.:—The Prophet Joseph's father; born at Topsfield, Essex Co., Mass., July 12, 1771; baptized April 6, 1830; ordained Patriarch to the Church, December 18, 1833; died in full fellowship in the Church at Nauvoo, Ill., Sept. 14, 1840.

Hyrum Smith:—Second son of Joseph Smith, Sen., born at Tunbridge, Vt. February 9, 1800; baptized June, 1829; appointed one of the First Presidency of the Church November 7, 1837; Patriarch to the Church January 19, 1841; martyred with his brother, the Prophet, at Carthage, Ill., June 27, 1844.

Samuel Harrison Smith:—Born Tunbridge, Vt., March 13, 1808; fourth son of Joseph Smith, Sen., baptized May 15, 1829; died July 30, 1844.

LECTURE II.

AUTHENTICITY OF THE BOOK OF MORMON.

1. The Divine Authenticity of the Book of Mormon constitutes our most important consideration of the work. This subject is one of vital interest to every earnest investigator of the ways of God, to every sincere searcher after truth. Claiming to be, as far as the present dispensation is conconcerned, a new scripture; presenting prophecies and revelations not heretofore recognized in modern theology; announcing to the world the message of a departed people; written by way of commandment, and by the spirit of prophecy and revelation; this volume is entitled to the most thorough and impartial examination. Nay, more, not alone does the Book of Mormon merit such consideration, it claims, even demands the same; for surely no one professing the most cursory belief in the power and authority of God can receive with unconcern the announcement of a new commandment, having the seal of Divine authority upon it. The question of the authenticity of the Book of Mormon is therefore one in which the world is interested.

2. The Latter-day Saints base their belief in the authenticity and genuineness of the book on the following proofs:—

I.   The general agreement of the Book of Mormon with the Bible.

II.   The fulfilment of ancient prophecies accomplished by the bringing forth of the Book of Mormon.

III.   The strict agreement and consistency of the Book of Mormon with itself.

IV.   The evident truth of its contained prophecies.

To these may be added certain external, or extra-scriptural evidences, amongst which are:—

V.   The strongly corroborative evidence furnished by modern discoveries in the field of archeological and ethnological science.

I. THE BOOK OF MORMON AND THE BIBLE.

3.   The Nephite and the Jewish Scriptures are found to agree in all matters of tradition, history, doctrine, and prophecy upon which both the separate records treat. These two volumes of scripture were prepared on opposite hemispheres, under conditions and circumstances widely diverse; yet between them there exists a surprising harmony, confirmatory of Divine inspiration in both.   The Book of Mormon contains a number of quotations from the ancient Jewish scriptures, a copy of which, as far as they had been compiled at the time of Lehi's exodus from Jerusalem, was brought to the western continent, as part of the record engraved on the plates of Laban.   In the case of such passages, there is no essential difference between Bible and Book of Mormon versions, except in instances of probable error in translation,—usually apparent through inconsistency or lack of clearness in the biblical reading.   There are, however, numerous minor variations in corresponding parts of the two volumes; and between such, examination usually demonstrates the superior perspicuity of the Nephite scripture.

4.   In a careful comparison of the prophecies of the Bible with corresponding predictions contained in the Book of Mormon, e. g. those relating to the birth, earthly ministry, sacrificial death, and second coming of Christ Jesus; others referring to the scattering and subsequent gathering of Israel; and such as relate to the establishment of Zion and the re-building of Jerusalem in the last days, each of the records will be seen to be corroborative of the other. True, there are many predictions in one which are not found in the other; but in no instance has a contradiction or an inconsistency between the two been pointed out. Between the doctrinal parts of the two volumes of scripture the same perfect harmony is found to prevail.

5. Of the agreement of the Book of Mormon with the Bible and with other standards of comparison, Apostle Orson Pratt has forcefully and truthfully written:—"If the miracles of the Book of Mormon be compared with the miracles of the Bible, there cannot be found in the former anything that would be more difficult to believe, than what we find in the latter. If we compare the historical, prophetical, and doctrinal parts of the Book of Mormon with the great truths of science and nature, we find no contradictions, no absurdities, nothing unreasonable. The most perfect harmony, therefore, exists between the great truths revealed in the Book of Mormon, and all other known truths, whether religious, historical, or scientific."[a]

II. ANCIENT PROPHECY REGARDING THE BOOK OF MORMON.

6. Ancient Prophecy has been literally fulfilled in the coming forth of the Book of Mormon. One of the earliest prophetic utterances directly bearing upon this subject is that of Enoch, the ante-diluvian prophet, unto whom the Lord revealed His purposes for all time. Witnessing in vision the corruption of mankind, after the ascension of the Son of Man, Enoch cried unto his God, "Wilt thou not come a̶̶̶ ̶̶on the earth?" "And the Lord said unto Enoch,

Authenticity of the Book of Mormon," Orson Pratt's Works, p. 236, .)

As I live, even so will I come in the last days. * * *
And the day shall come that the earth shall rest, but before
that day the heavens shall be darkened, and a veil of darkness shall cover the earth, and the heavens shall shake and
also the earth, and great tribulations shall be among the
children of men; but my people will I preserve, and righteousness will I send down out of heaven, and truth will I
send forth out of the earth, to bear testimony of Mine Only
Begotten. * * * and righteousness and truth will I
cause to sweep the earth as with a flood to gather out mine
own elect from the four quarters of the earth, unto a place
which I shall prepare."[b] The Latter-day Saints regard
the coming forth of the Book of Mormon, together with the
restoration of the Priesthood by the direct ministration of
heavenly messengers, as a fulfilment of this prophecy, and
of similar predictions contained in the Bible.

7. **Biblical Prophecies and their Fulfilment:**—David, who
sang his psalms over a thousand years before the "Meridian
of Time," declared, "Truth shall spring out of the earth,
and righteousness shall look down from heaven."[c] And so
also declared Isaiah.[d] Ezekiel saw in vision[e] the coming
together of the stick of Judah, and the stick of Joseph,
signifying, as the Latter-day Saints affirm, the Bible and
the Book of Mormon. The passage last referred to reads,
in the words of Ezekiel:—"The word of the Lord came
again unto me, saying, Moreover, thou son of man, take
thee one stick, and write upon it, For Judah, and for the
children of Israel his companions: then take another stick,
and write upon it, For Joseph, the stick of Ephraim, and
for all the house of Israel his companions: And join them

---

b Pearl of Great Price. Writings of Moses, p. 44. (1888 ed.)
c Psalms lxxxv, 11.
d Isa. xlv, 8.
e Ezek. xxxvii, particularly verses 15-20.

one to another into one stick; and they shall become one in thine hand."

8. When we call to mind the ancient custom in the making of books,—that of writing on long strips of parchment and rolling the same on rods or sticks, the use of the word "stick" as equivalent to "book" in the passage becomes at once apparent.[f] At the time of this utterance, the Israelites had divided into two nations known as the people of Judah, and that of Israel, or Ephraim. There would seem to be little room for doubt that the records of Judah and of Joseph are here referred to.[g] Now, as we have seen, the Nephite nation comprised the descendants of Lehi of the tribe of Manasseh, of Ishmael an Ephraimite, and of Zoram whose tribal relation is not definitely stated. The Nephites were then of the tribes of Joseph; and their record or "stick" is as truly represented by the Book of Mormon as is the "stick" of Judah by the Bible.

9. That the coming forth of the record of Joseph or Ephraim is to be accomplished through the direct power of God is evident from the Lord's interpretation of the vision of Ezekiel, wherein He says:—"Behold, *I will take* the stick of Joseph * * * and will put them with him, even with the stick of Judah."[h] And that this union of the two records is to be a characteristic of the latter days is evident from the prediction of an event which is to follow immediately, viz., the gathering of the tribes from the nations among which they had been dispersed.[i] Comparison with other prophecies relating to the gathering will conclusively prove that the great event is to take place in the latter times, preparatory to the second coming of Christ.[j]

---

[f] See a corresponding use of the word "roll" in Jeremiah xxxvi, 1, 2; and its synonym "book" in verses 8, 10, 11, and 13.

[g] Compare with Lehi's prediction made to his son Joseph, II Nephi iii, 12.

[h] Ezek. xxxvii, 19.

[i] Verse 21.

[j] See lecture on "Gathering" in connection with Article 10, "Articles of Faith."

10.   Reverting to the writings of Isaiah, we find that prophet voicing the Lord's threatenings against Ariel, or Jerusalem, "the city where David dwelt." Ariel was to be distressed, burdened with heaviness and sorrow; then the prophet refers to some people, other than Judah who occupied Jerusalem, for he makes comparison with the latter, saying "And it shall be unto me *as* Ariel." As to the fate decreed against this other people we read:—"And thou shalt be brought down, and shalt speak out of the ground, and thy speech shall be low out of the dust, and thy voice shall be, as of one that hath a familiar spirit, out of the ground, and thy speech shall whisper out of the dust."[k]

11.   Of the fulfilment of these and associated prophecies, a modern apostle has written:—"These predictions of Isaiah could not refer to Ariel, or Jerusalem, because their speech has not been 'out of the ground,' or 'low out of the dust;' but it refers to the remnant of Joseph who were destroyed in America upwards of fourteen hundred years ago. The Book of Mormon describes their downfall, and truly it was great and terrible. At the crucifixion of Christ, 'the multitude of their terrible ones,' as Isaiah predicted, 'became as chaff that passeth away,' and it took place as he further predicts, 'at an instant suddenly.' * * * This remnant of Joseph in their distress and destruction became *as* Ariel. As the Roman army lay siege to Ariel, and brought upon her great distress and sorrow, so did the contending nations of ancient America bring upon each other the most direful scenes of blood and carnage. Therefore, the Lord could, with the greatest propriety, when speaking in reference to this event, declare that, 'It shall be unto me *as* Ariel.'"[l]

12.   Isaiah's striking prediction that the nation thus

---

k Isaiah xxix, 4—read verses 1-6.

l Orson Pratt, *Divine Authenticity of the Book of Mormon*, p.p. 293-294 (Utah ed. 1891). For details of fulfilment of part of the prophecy, see III Nephi viii-ix.

brought down should "speak out of the ground," with speech "low out of the dust" was literally fulfilled in the bringing forth of the Book of Mormon, the original of which was taken out of the ground, and the voice of the record is as that of one speaking from the dust. In continuation of the same prophecy we read:—"And the vision of all is become unto you as the words of a book that is sealed, which men deliver unto one that is learned, saying, Read this, I pray thee: and he saith, I cannot; for it is sealed: And the book is delivered unto him that is not learned, saying, Read this, I pray thee: and he saith, I am not learned."[m] The fulfilment of this prediction is claimed in the presentation of the transcript from the plates,—"the words of a book," not the book itself, to the learned Prof. Anthon, whose reply almost in the words of the text has been cited;[n] and in the delivery of the book itself to the unlettered lad, Joseph Smith.

III. CONSISTENCY OF STYLE AND MATTER IN THE BOOK
OF MORMON.

13. **The Consistency of the Book of Mormon** sustains belief in its Divine origin. The parts bear evidence of having been written at different times, and under widely varying conditions. The style of the component books is in harmony with the times and circumstances of their production. The portions which were transcribed from the plates bearing Mormon's abridgment contain numerous interpolations as comments and explanations of the transcriber; but in the first six books, which, as already explained, are the verbatim record of the smaller plates of Nephi, no such interpolations occur. The book maintains strict consistency through-

---

m Isaiah xxix, 11-12.
n See p. 273-274.

out all its parts; no contradictions, no disagreements have
been pointed out.

14. A Marked Diversity of Style characterizes the several
parts.° From what has been said regarding the classes of
plates which constitute the original records of the Book of
Mormon, it is evident that the volume contains the compiled writings of a long line of inspired scribes extending
through a thousand years, this time-range being exclusive of
the earlier years of Jaredite history. Unity of style is not
to be expected under such conditions, and indeed, did such
occur, it would be fatal to the claims made for the volume.

IV. THE BOOK OF MORMON SUSTAINED BY THE FULFIL-
    MENT OF ITS CONTAINED PROPHECIES.

15. Book of Mormon Predictions are numerous and important. Amongst the most conclusive proofs of the
authenticity of the book is that furnished by the demonstrated truth of its contained prophecies. Prophecy is
best proved in the light of its own fulfilment. The predictions contained within the Book of Mormon may be
classed as (a) Prophecies relating to the time covered by
the book itself, the fulfilment of which is recorded therein;
and, (b) Prophecies relating to times beyond the limits of
the history chronicled in the book.

16. *Prophecies of the First Class* named, the fulfilment
of which is attested by the Book of Mormon record, are of
but minor value as proof of the authenticity of the work;
for, had the book been written according to a plot devised
by man, both prediction and fulfilment would have been
provided for with equal care and ingenuity. Nevertheless,
to the studious and conscientious reader, the genuineness
of the book will be apparent; and the account of the
literal realization of the numerous and varied predictions

o See Note 1.

relating to the fate then future of the people whose history
is given in the record, as also of those concerning the details of the birth and death of the Savior, and of His
appearing in a resurrected state, must, by their accuracy
and consistency, appeal with force as evidence of inspiration and authority in the record.

17. *Prophecies of the Second Class*, relating to a time
which to the writers was far future, are numerous and ex-
plicit: many of them have special reference to the last days,
—the dispensation of the fulness of times,—and of these,
some have been already strictly accomplished, others are
now in process of actual realization, while yet others are
awaiting fulfilment under specified conditions which seem
now to be rapidly approaching. Among the most remarkable of the Book of Mormon predictions incident to the last
dispensation are those that relate to its own coming forth
and the effect of its publication amongst mankind. Ezekiel's biblical prophecy concerning the coming together of
the "sticks," or records, of Judah and of Ephraim has
received attention; consider a like prediction pronounced as
a blessing by Lehi upon the head of his son Joseph, which
couples the prophecy concerning the book with that of the
seer through whose instrumentality the miracle was to be
accomplished:—"But a seer will I raise up out of the fruit
of thy loins; and unto him will I give power to bring forth
my word unto the seed of thy loins; and not to the bringing
forth my word only, saith the Lord, but to the convincing
them of my word, which shall have already gone forth
among them. Wherefore, the fruit of thy loins shall write;
and the fruit of the loins of Judah shall write; and that
which shall be written by the fruit of thy loins, and also
that which shall be written by the fruit of the loins of
Judah, shall grow together, unto the confounding of false
doctrines, and laying down of contentions, and establishing

3

peace among the fruit of thy loins, and bringing them to
the knowledge of their fathers in the latter days; and also to
the knowledge of my covenants, saith the Lord.   And out
of weakness he shall be made strong, in that day when my
work shall commence among all my people, unto the restor-
ing thee, O house of Israel, saith the Lord."*p*   The literal
fulfilment of these utterances in the bringing forth of the
Book of Mormon through Joseph Smith is of itself apparent.

18.   Unto Nephi the Lord showed the effect of the new
publication; declaring that in the day of Israel's gathering,
—plainly then the day of the fulness of times, as attested
by the Jewish scriptures,—the words of the Nephites should
be given to the world, and should "hiss forth unto the ends
of the earth, for a standard" unto the house of Israel; and
that then the Gentiles, forgetting even their debt to the
Jews from whom they have received the Bible in which they
profess such faith, would revile and curse that branch of the
covenant people, and would reject the new scripture, ex-
claiming, "A Bible! a Bible! we have got a Bible, and there
cannot be any more Bible."*q*   Is this not the burden of the
frenzied objections raised by the Gentile world against the
Book of Mormon,—that it is of necessity void because new
revelation is not to be expected?

19.   Now, in olden times, two witnesses were required to
establish the truth of any allegation; and, says the Lord
concerning the dual records witnessing of Himself:—"Wherefore murmur ye, because that ye shall receive more of my
word?   Know ye not that the testimony of two nations is a
witness unto you that I am God, that I remember one nation
like unto another?   Wherefore, I speak the same words unto
one nation like unto another.   And when the two nations

p II Nephi iii, 11-13.
q II Nephi xxix, 3; read the chapter.

shall run together, the testimony of the two nations shall run together also."[r]

20. Associated with these predictions of the joint testimony of Jewish and Nephite scriptures, is another prophecy, the consummation of which is now eagerly awaited by the faithful. Other scriptures are promised; note this word of God:—"Wherefore, because that ye have a Bible, ye need not suppose that it contains all my words; neither need ye suppose that I have not caused more to be written: * * * * * For behold, I shall speak unto the Jews, and they shall write it; and I shall also speak unto the Nephites, and they shall write it; and I shall also speak unto the other tribes of the house of Israel, which I have led away, and they shall write it; and I shall also speak unto all nations of the earth, and they shall write it. And it shall come to pass that the Jews shall have the words of the Nephites, and the Nephites shall have the words of the Jews; and the Nephites and the Jews shall have the words of the lost tribes of Israel; and the lost tribes of Israel shall have the words of the Nephites and the Jews."[s]

V. CORROBORATIVE EVIDENCE FURNISHED BY MODERN DISCOVERIES.

21. **The Archeology and Ethnology** of the western continent contribute valuable corroborative evidence in support of the Book of Mormon. These sciences are confessedly unable to explain in any decisive manner the origin of the native American races; nevertheless, investigation in this field has yielded some results that are fairly definite, and with the most important of these the Book of Mormon account is in general accord. Among the most prominent

---

[r] Verse 8.
[s] Verses 10 and 12.

of the discoveries respecting the aboriginal inhabitants, are the following:—

I.   That America was inhabited in very ancient times, probably soon after the building of the Tower of Babel.

II.   That the continent has been successively occupied by different peoples, at least by two classes, or so-called "races" at widely separated periods.

III.   That the aboriginal inhabitants came from the east, probably from Asia, and that the later occupants, or those of the second period, were closely allied to, if not identical with, the Israelites.

IV.   That the existing native races of America have sprung from a common stock.

22.   From the outline already given of the historical part of the Book of Mormon, it is seen that each of these discoveries is fully attested by that record.   Thus it is stated therein:—

I.   That America was settled by the Jaredites, who came direct from the scenes of Babel.

II.   That the Jaredites occupied the land for about eighteen hundred and fifty years, during which time they spread over a great part of North and South America; and that at about the time of their extinction (near 590 B. C.), Lehi and his company came to this continent where they developed into the segregated nations Nephites and Lamanites; the former becoming extinct near 385 A. D., about a thousand years after Lehi's arrival on these shores; the latter continuing in a degenerate condition until the present, being represented by the Indian tribes of today.

III.   That Lehi, Ishmael, and Zoram, the progenitors of both Nephites and Lamanites, were undoubtedly Israelites, Lehi being of the tribe of Manasseh while Ishmael was an Ephraimite; and that the colony came direct from Jerusalem, in Asia.

IV.   That the existing Indian tribes are all direct descendants of Lehi and his company, and that therefore they have sprung from men all of whom were of the house of Israel.

Now let us examine some of the evidence bearing on these points presented by individual investigators, most of whom knew nothing of the Book of Mormon, and none of whom accept the book as authentic.[t]

23. I. Concerning the very Ancient Period at which America was Inhabited:—A recognized authority on American antiquities gives the following evidence and inference:—"One of the arts known to the builders of Babel was that of brick making. This art was also known to the people who built the works in the west. The knowledge of copper was known to the people of the plains of Shinar; for Noah must have communicated it, as he lived a hundred and fifty years among them after the flood. Also copper was known to the ante-diluvians. Copper was also known to the authors of the western monuments. Iron was known to the ante-diluvians. It was also known to the ancients of the west. However, it is evident that very little iron was among them, as very few instances of its discovery in their works have occurred; and for this very reason we draw a conclusion that they came to this country soon after the dispersion."[u]

24. Lowry, in his "Reply to official inquiries respecting the Aborigines of America," concludes concerning the peopling of the western continent, "that the first settlement

[t] Acknowledgments:—Many of the citations which follow, used in connection with the extra-scriptural evidence supporting the Book of Mormon, have been brought together by writers among our people, particularly by Elder George Reynolds; (see his lectures as specified where quoted); also series of articles entitled "American Antiquities," in Millennial Star, Liverpool, vol. xxi: by Moses Thatcher, (See a series of articles on "The Divine Origin of the Book of Mormon," in Contributor, Salt Lake City, vol. II;) and by Elder Edwin F. Parry; (see tract, "A Prophet of Latter-days;" Liverpool, 1898.)

[u] Priest, *American Antiquities*. (1833).

was made shortly after the confusion of tongues at the building of the Tower of Babel."[v]

25. Prof. Waterman of Boston says of the progenitors of the American Indians:—"When and whence did they come? Albert Galatin, one of the profoundest philologists of the age, concluded, that, so far as language afforded any clue, the time of their arrival could not have been long after the dispersion of the human family."[w]

26. Pritchard says of America's ancient inhabitants, that, "the era of their existence as a distinct and isolated race must probably be dated as far back as that time which separated into nations the inhabitants of the old world, and gave to each branch of the human family its primitive language and individuality."[x]

27. A native Mexican author, Ixtilxochitl, "fixes the date of the first peopling of America about the year 2000 B. C.; this closely accords with that given by the Book of Mormon, which positively declares that it occurred at the time of the dispersion, when God in His anger scattered the people upon the face of the whole earth."[v] "Referring to the quotations from Ixtilxochitl, seventeen hundred and sixteen years are said to have elapsed from the creation to the flood. Moses places it sixteen hundred and fifty-six, a difference of only sixty years.[z] They agree exactly as to the number of cubits, fifteen, which the waters prevailed over the highest mountains. Such a coincidence can lead to but one conclusion, the identity of origin of the two accounts."[a]

v Schoolcraft's *Ethnological Researches*, vol. iii, (1853.)

w Extract from lecture by Prof. Waterman, delivered in Bristol, England, 1849; quoted in pamphlet by Edwin F. Parry *"A Prophet of Latter Days,"* (Liverpool, 1898.)

x Pritchard, *National History of Man*, (London, 1845.)

y Moses Thatcher, *Contributor*, vol. ii, p. 227, Salt Lake City, 1881.

z See Note 2.

a Moses Thatcher, *Contributor*, vol. ii, p. 228.

28.   Prof. Short, quoting from Clavigero, says, "The Chiapanese have been the first peoplers of the New World, if we give credit to their traditions.   They say that Votan, the grandson of that respectable old man who built the great ark to save himself and family from the deluge, and one of those who undertook the building of that lofty edifice, which was to reach up to heaven, went by express command of the Lord to people that land.   They say also that the first people came from the quarter of the north, and that when they arrived at Soconusco, they separated, some going to inhabit the country of Nicaragua, and others remaining at Chiapas."[a]

29.   **II. Concerning the Successive Occupation of America by Different Peoples in Ancient Times:**—It has been declared by eminent students of American archeology, that two distinct classes, by some designated as separate races, of mankind inhabited this continent in early times: Prof. F. W. Putnam[b] is even more definite in his assertion that one of these ancient races spread from the north, the other from the south.   This is in agreement with the Book of Mormon record, which describes the occupation of the continent by the Jaredites and the Nephites in turn, the former having established themselves first in North America, the latter in South America.   H. C. Walsh, in an article entitled "Copan, a City of the Dead,"[c] gives many interesting details of excavation and other work prosecuted by Gordon under the auspices of the Peabody expedition; and adds, "All this points to successive periods of occupation, of which there are other evidences."[d]

---

a John T. Short, *North Americans of Antiquity*, p. 204. (Harper Bros., New York; 2nd ed. 1888.) See also *Contributor*, (Salt Lake City; vol. II, p. 259).

b Putnam, "*Prehistoric Remains in the Ohio Valley*," Century Magazine, March, 1890.

c See *Harper's Weekly*, (New York,) October, 1897; article by Henry C. Walsh.

d See note 3

30. III. Concerning the Advent of at least One Division of the Ancient Americans from the East, probably from Asia; and their Israelitish Origin:—Comfirmatory evidence of the belief that the aboriginal Americans sprang from the peoples of the eastern hemisphere is found in the similarity of record and tradition on the two continents, regarding the creation, the deluge, and other great events of history. Boturini[f] who is quoted by most writers on American archeology says, "There is no Gentile nation that refers to primitive events with such certainty as the Indians do. They give us an account of the creation of the world, of the deluge,[g] of the confusion of languages at the Tower of Babel, and of all other periods and ages of the world, and of the long peregrinations which their people had in Asia, representing the specific years by their characters; and in the seven Conejos (rabbits) they tell us of the great eclipse that occurred at the death of Christ, our Lord."

31. Similar evidence of the common source of eastern and western traditions of great events in primitive times is furnished in the writings of Short, already quoted, and by Baldwin,[h] Clavigero,[i] Kingsborough,[j] Sahagun,[k] Prescott,[l] Schoolcraft,[m] Squiers,[n] Adair,[o] and others.[p]

32. Prof. Short adds his testimony to the evidence of the

---

f Chevalier Boturini; he spent several years investigating the antiquities of Mexico and Central America, and collected many valuable records, of most of which he was despoiled by the Spanish; he published a work on the subject of his studies in 1746.

g See Note 4.

h Baldwin, "*Ancient America*," (Harper Bros., New York, 1871.)

i Clavigero, quoted by Prof. Short in "*North Americans of Antiquity*."

j Lord Kingsborough, "*Mexican Antiquities*" (1830-37.)

k Bernardo de Sahagun, "*Historia Universal de Nueva Espana*."

l W. H. Prescott, "*Conquest of Mexico*" (see pp. 463-4.)

m Schoolcraft, "*Ethnological Researches*," (1851); see vol. i.

n Squiers, "*Antiquities of the State of New York*," 1851.

o Adair, "*History of the American Indians*," London, 1775.

p See Bancroft's "*Native Races*," etc, vols. iii and v; Donelly's "*Atlantis*," p 391, (1882.)

aboriginal inhabitants of America being of "Old World origin," but admits his inability to determine when or whence they came to this continent.[q] Waterman, before cited, says: "This people could not have been created in Africa, for its inhabitants were widely dissimilar from those of America; nor in Europe, which was without a native people agreeing at all with American races; then to Asia alone could they look for the origin of the Americans."[r]

33. It has been demonstrated that the aboriginal tribes were accustomed to practice under certain conditions the rites of circumcision,[s] baptism, and animal sacrifice.[t] Herrera, a Spanish writer of three centuries ago, states that among the primitive inhabitants of Yucatan baptism was known by a name that meant to be born again.[u] An interesting discovery of an engraved stone presenting a record of the ten commandments has been reported from the Indian mounds of Ohio."[v]

34. But it is not alone in the matter of custom and tradition relating to pre-Christian times that so marked a resemblance is found between the peoples of the old and the new world. Many traditions and some records, telling of the pre-destined Christ and His atoning death, were current among the native races of this continent long prior to the advent of Christian discoverers in recent centuries. Indeed, when the Spaniards first invaded Mexico, their Catholic priests found a native knowledge of Christ and the Godhead, so closely corresponding with the doctrines of ortho-

q John T. Short, *North Americans of Antiquity,* (1888.)

r Extract from lecture by Prof. Waterman, delivered in Bristol, England, 1849; quoted in pamphlet by Edwin F. Parry, *"A Prophet of Latter-days,"* Liverpool, 1898.

s Lord Kingsborough.

t Donelly's *"Atlantis,"* p. 144.

u Tract *"A Prophet of Latter-days,"* by Edwin F. Parry, p. 106.

v See an article by Elder George Reynolds, in *"Contributor"* (Salt Lake City), xvii, pp. 233.

dox Christianity, that they, in their inability to account for the same, invented the theory that Satan had planted among the natives of the country, an imitation gospel for the purpose of deluding the people. A rival theory held that Thomas, the apostle, had visited the western continent, and had taught the gospel of Christ.[w]

35. Lord Kingsborough, in his comprehensive and standard work, refers to a manuscript by Las Casas the Spanish Bishop of Chiapa, which writing is preserved in the convent of St. Dominic; in this the Bishop states that a very accurate knowledge of the Godhead was found to exist among the natives of Yucatan. One of the bishop's emissaries wrote that "he had met with a principal lord, who informed him that they believed in God, who resided in heaven, even the Father, the Son, and the Holy Spirit. The Father was named Yeona, the Son Bahab, who was born of a virgin, named Chibirias, and that the Holy Spirit was called Euach. Bahab, the Son, they said, was put to death by Eupuro, who scourged Him, and put on his head a crown of thorns, and placed Him with His arms stretched upon a beam of wood; and that, on the third day, He came to life, and ascended into heaven, where He is with the Father; that immediately after, the Euach came as a merchant, bringing precious merchandise, filling those who would with gifts and graces, abundant and divine."[x]

36. Rosales affirms a tradition among the Chileans to the effect that their forefathers were visited by a wonderful personage, full of grace and power, who wrought many miracles among them, and taught them of the Creator who dwelt in heaven in the midst of glorified hosts.[y] Prescott refers to the symbol of the cross which was found by the

w See Pres. John Taylor's *Mediation and Atonement*, p. 201.

x Kingsborough's *Antiquities of Mexico.*

y Rosales, *History of Chile.* See Prest. Taylor's *Mediation and Atonement*, p. 202.

Catholics who accompanied Cortez, to be common among the natives of Mexico and Central America. In addition to this sign of a belief in Christ, a ceremony akin to that of the Lord's Supper was witnessed with astonishment by the invaders. The Aztec priests were seen to prepare a cake of flour, mixed with blood, which they consecrated and distributed among the people, who as they ate, "showed signs of humiliation and sorrow, declaring it was the flesh of Deity."[z]

37. The Mexicans recognize a Deity in Quetzalcoatl, the traditional account of whose life and death is closely akin to our history of the Christ, so that, says President John Taylor, "we can come to no other conclusion than that Quetzalcoatl and Christ are the same being."[a] Lord Kingsborough speaks of a painting of Quetzalcoatl, "in the attitude of a person crucified, with the impression of nails in his hands and feet, but not actually upon the cross." The same authority further says, "The seventy-third plate of the Borgian MS. is the most remarkable of all, for Quetzalcoatl is not only represented there as crucified upon a cross of Greek form, but his burial and descent into hell are also depicted in a very curious manner." And again:— "The Mexicans believe that Quetzalcoatl took human nature upon him, partaking of all the infirmities of man, and was not exempt from sorrow, pain or death, which he suffered voluntarily to atone for the sins of man."[b]

38. The source of this knowledge of Christ and the God-head, to account for which gave such trouble to the Catholic invaders and caused them to resort to extreme and un-founded theory, is plainly apparent to the student of the Book of Mormon. We learn from that sacred scripture,

z Prescott, *Conquest of Mexico*, p. 465.
a *Mediation and Atonement*, p. 201; See Note 5.
b Lord Kingsborough, *Antiquities of Mexico;* see quotations by Pres. John Taylor, *Mediation and Atonement*, p. 202.

that the progenitors of the native American races, for centuries prior to the time of Christ's birth, lived in the light
of direct revelation, which, coming to them through their
authorized prophets, showed the purposes of God respecting
the redemption of mankind; and, moreover, that the risen
Redeemer ministered unto them in person, and established
His Church among them with all its essential ordinances.
The people have fallen into a state of spiritual degeneracy;
many of their traditions are sadly distorted, and disfigured
by admixture of superstition and human invention; yet the
origin of their knowledge is plainly authentic.

39. IV. Concerning the Common Origin of the Native
Races on this Continent:—That the many tribes and nations
among the Indians and other "native races" of America
are of common parentage is very generally admitted; the
conclusion is based on the evident close relationship in
their languages, traditions, and customs. "Mr. Lewis H.
Morgan finds evidence that the American aborigines had a
common origin in what he calls 'their system of consan-
guinity and affinity.' He says, 'The Indian nations from
the Atlantic to the Rocky Mountains, and from the Arctic
sea to the Gulf of Mexico, with the exception of the
Esquimaux, have the same system. It is elaborate and
complicated in its general form and details; and, while
deviations from uniformity occur in the systems of different
stocks, the radical feature, are in the main constant. This
identity in the essential characteristics of a system so remarkable tends to show that it must have been transmitted
with the blood to each stock from a common original
source. It affords the strongest evidence yet obtained of
unity in origin of the Indian nations within the regions
defined.' "[c]

---

c Baldwin's "Ancient America," p. 56; see citations of conclusions regarding
the characteristics of aboriginal Americans by Bradford, in the same work.

40. Baldwin further quotes Bradford's summary of conclusions regarding the origin and characteristics of the
ancient Americans, amongst which we read:—"That they
were all of the same origin, branches of the same race, and
possessed of similar customs and institutions."[d]   Adair
writes:—"All the various nations of Indians seem to be of
one descent;" and, in support of this conclusion he pre-
sents abundant evidence of similarity of language, habits,
and customs; religious ceremonies; modes of administering
justice, etc.[e]

41. **Written Language of the Ancient Americans:**—To
these secular, or extra-scriptural, evidences of the authenticity of the Book of Mormon, may be added the agreement
of the record with recent discoveries regarding the written
language of these ancient peoples.   The prophet Nephi
states that he made his record on the plates in "the language
of the Egyptians,"[f] and we are further told that the brazen
plates of Laban were inscribed in the same.[g]   Mormon, who
abridged the voluminous writings of his predecessors, and
prepared the plates from which the modern translation was
made, employed also the Egyptian characters.   His son
Moroni, who completed the record, declares this fact; but,
recognizing a difference between the writing of his day and
that on the earlier plates, he attributed the change to the
natural mutation through time, and speaks of his own
record and that of his father, Mormon, as being written in
the "reformed Egyptian."[h]

42. Now consider the testimony of Dr. Le Plongeon,
announcing his discovery of a sacred alphabet among the
Mayas of Central America, which he declares to be practi-

---

d The same.
e Adair's "*History of the American Indians,*" London, 1775.
f I Nephi i, 2.
g Mosiah i, 4.
h Mormon ix, 32.

cally identical with the Egyptian alphabet. He states that the structure of the Maya sacred language closely resembles that of the Egyptians; and he boldly proclaims his conviction that the two nations derived their written language from the same source.[i] Another authority says:—"The eye of the antiquarian cannot fail to be both attracted and fixed by evidence of the existence of two great branches of the hieroglyphical language,—both having striking affinities with the Egyptian, and yet distinguished from it by characteristics perfectly American."[j]

43. But the Egyptian is not the only eastern language found to be represented in the relics of American antiquities; the Hebrew occurs in this connection with at least equal significance. That the Hebrew tongue should have been used by Lehi's descendents is most natural, inasmuch as they were of the House of Israel, transferred to the western continent directly from Jerusalem. That the ability to read and write in that language continued with the Nephites until the time of their extinction, is evident from Moroni's statement regarding the language used on the plates of Mormon:—"And now behold, we have written this record according to our knowledge, in the characters which are called among us the reformed Egyptian, being handed down and altered by us according to our manner of speech. And if our plates had been sufficiently large, we should have written in Hebrew; but the Hebrew hath been altered by us also."[k] Many discoveries of engravings and writings in changed Hebrew characters have been reported from various American localities; and a corrupted form of Hebrew has been recognized among the spoken language of some of the native races.

i Dr. August Le Plongeon, in *Review* of *Reviews*, July, 1895.

j "*Quarterly Review*," October. 1836; abstracted in "*Millennial Star*," vol. xxi. p. 467.

k Mormon ix, 32-33.

44. The following instances are taken from an instructive array of such, brought together by Elder George Reynolds.[l] Several of the early Spanish writers claim that the natives of some portions of the land were found speaking a corrupt Hebrew. "Las Casas so affirms with regard to the inhabitants of the island of Hayti. Lafitu wrote a history wherein he maintained that the Carribee language was radically Hebrew. Isaac Nasci, a learned Jew of Surinam, says of the language of the people of Guiana, that all their substantives are Hebrew." Spanish historians record the early discovery of Hebrew characters on the western continent. "Malvenda says that the natives of St. Michael had tombstones, which the Spaniards digged up, with several ancient Hebrew inscriptions upon them." Between 1860 and 1865, four stones engraved with Hebrew inscriptions were found in different parts of Ohio. One of these bore an engraved inscription in Hebrew of the Ten Commandments in an abridged form.[m] Parchments have also been found, bearing in Hebrew characters texts from the ancient scriptures.

45. In all such writings, the characters and the language are allied to the most ancient form of Hebrew, and show none of the vowel signs and terminal letters which were introduced into the Hebrew of the eastern continent after the return of the Jews from the Babylonian captivity. This is consistent with the fact that Lehi and his people left Jerusalem shortly before the captivity, and therefore prior to the introduction of the changes in the written language.

46. **Another Test:**—Let not the reader of the Book of Mormon content himself with such evidences as have been cited concerning the Divine authenticity of this reputed scripture. There is promised a surer and a more effectual

l Reynolds' lecture, "*The Language of the Book of Mormon.*"
m See page 297.

means of ascertaining the truth or falsity of this marvelous volume. Like other scriptures, the Book of Mormon is to be comprehended through the spirit of the scriptures, and this is obtainable only as a gift from God. But this gift, priceless though it be, is promised unto all who would seek for it. Then to all let us commend the counsel of the last writer in the volume, Moroni, the solitary scribe who sealed the book, afterward the angel of the record who brought it forth:—"And when ye shall receive these things, I would exhort you that ye would ask God, the Eternal Father, in the name of Christ, if these things are not true; and if ye shall ask with a sincere heart, with real intent, having faith in Christ, he will manifest the truth of it unto you, by the power of the Holy Ghost; and by the power of the Holy Ghost ye may know the truth of all things.'"[n]

NOTES:

1. **Diversity of Literary Style in the Book of Mormon:**—"There is a marked difference in the literary style of Nephi and some of the other earlier prophets from that of Mormon and Moroni. Mormon and his son are more direct and take fewer words to express their ideas than did the earlier writers, at least their manner is, to most readers, the more pleasing. Amos, the son of Jacob, has also a style peculiar to himself. There is another noticable fact that when original records or discourses, such as the record of Limhi, the sermons of Alma, Amulek, etc., the epistles of Helaman, and others, are introduced into Mormon's abridgment, words and expressions are used that appear nowhere else in the Book of Mormon. This diversity of style, expression, and wording is a very pleasing incidental testimony to the truth of the claim made for the Book of Mormon,—that it is a compilation of the work of many writers."—From Lectures on the Book of Mormon, by Elder George Reynolds.

2. **Mexican Date of the Deluge:**—In speaking of the time of the Deluge as given by the Mexican author, Ixtilxochitl, Elder George Reynolds says:— "There is a remarkable agreement between this writer's statements and the Book of Genesis. The time from the Fall to the Flood only differs sixty, possibly only five years, if the following statement in the Book of Doctrine and Covenants (cvii, 49) regarding Enoch lengthens the chronology: "And he saw the Lord, and he walked with him, and was before his face continually; and he walked with God 365 years, making him 430 years old when he was translated." The same statement is made in the Pearl of Great Price, page 45, (1888 ed.)—

----

[n] Moroni x. 4-5.

From lecture on *External Evidences of the Book of Mormon.* by Elder Geo. Reynolds.

3. Ancient Civilization in America:—"That a civilization once flourished in these regions [Central America and Mexico] much higher than any the Spanish conquerors found upon their arrival, there can be no doubt. By far the most important work that has been done among the remains of the old Maya civilization has been carried on by the Peabody Museum of Harvard College, through a series of expeditions it has sent to the buried city now called Copan, in Spanish Honduras. In a beautiful valley near the borderland of Guatemala, surrounded by steep mountains and watered by a winding river, the hoary city lies wrapped in the sleep of ages. The ruins at Copan, although in a more advanced state of destruction than those of the Maya cities of Yucatan, have a general similarity to the latter in the design of the buildings, and in the sculptures, while the characters in the inscriptions are essentially the same. It would seem, therefore, that Copan was a city of the Mayas; but if so it must have been one of their most ancient settlements, fallen into decay long before the cities of Yucatan reached their prime. The Maya civilization was totally distinct from the Aztec or Mexican; it was an older and also a much higher civilization."—Henry C. Walsh, in article "*Copan, a City of the Dead,*" Harpers' Weekly, October, 1897.

Baldwin, in his valuable work "Ancient America" incorporates the conclusions announced by Bradford in regard to the ancient occupants of North America, as follows:—

"That they were all of the same origin, branches of the same race, and possessed of similar customs and institutions.

"That they were populous, and occupied a great extent of territory.

"That they had arrived at a considerable degree of civilization, were associated in large communities, and lived in extensive cities.

"That they possessed the use of many of the metals, such as lead, copper, gold, and silver, and probably the art of working in them.

"That they sculptured in stone, and sometimes used that material in the construction of their edifices.

"That they had the knowledge of the arch of receding steps; of the art of pottery, producing urns and utensils formed with taste, and constructed upon the principles of chemical composition; and the art of brick-making.

"That they worked the salt springs, and manufactured salt.

"That they were an agricultural people, living under the influence and protection of regular forms of governments.

"That they possessed a decided system of religion, and a mythology connected with astronomy, which, with its sister science, geometry, was in the hands of the priesthood.

"That they were skilled in the art of fortification.

"That the epoch of their original settlement in the United States is of great antiquity; and that the only indications of their origin to be gathered from the locality of their ruined monuments, point toward Mexico."—Baldwin, *Ancient America*, p. 56.

4. American Traditions Concerning the Deluge:—"Don Francisco Munoz de la Vega, the Bishop of that diocese (Chiapas),certifies in the prologue to his 'Diocesan Constitutions,' declaring that an ancient manuscript of the primitive Indians of that province, who had learned the art of writing, was in his record office, who retained the constant tradition that the father and founder of

3

their nation was named Teponahuale, which signifies lord of the hollow piece of wood: and that he was present at the building of the Great Wall, for so they named the Tower of Babel; and beheld with his own eyes the confusion of language; after which event, God, the Creator, commanded him to come to these extensive regions, and to divide them amongst mankind.—Lord Kingsborough, *Mexican Antiquities*, vol. viii, p. 25.

"It is found in the histories of the Toltecs that this age and first world, as they call it, lasted 1716 years: that men were destroyed by tremendous rains and lightnings from the sky, and even all the land, without the exception of anything, and the highest mountains, were covered up and submerged in water fifteen cubits (caxtolmolatli); and here they added other fables of how men came to multiply from the few who escaped from this destruction in a 'toptlipetlocali;' that this word nearly signifies a close chest; and how, after men had multiplied, they erected a very high 'zacuali,'which is today a tower of great height, in order to take refuge in it should the second world (age) be destroyed. Presently their languages were confused, and, not being able to understand each other, they went to different parts of the earth."—The same, vol. ix, p. 321.

"The most important among the American traditions are the Mexican, for they appear to have been definitely fixed by symbolic and mnemonic paintings before any contact with Europeans. According to these documents, the Noah of the Mexican cataclysm was Coxcox, called by certain people Teocipactli or Tezpi. He had saved himself, together with his wife Xochiquetzal, in a bark, or, according to other traditions, on a raft made of cypress-wood, (*Cypressus disticha*). Paintings retracing the deluge of Coxcox have been discovered among the Aztecs, Miztecs, Zapotecs, Tlascaltecs, and Mechoacaneses. The tradition of the latter is still more strikingly in conformity with the story as we have it in Genesis, and in Chaldean sources. It tells how Tezpi embarked in a spacious vessel with his wife, his children, and several animals, and grain, whose preservation was essential to the subsistence of the human race. When the great god Tezcatlipoca decreed that the waters should retire, Tezpi sent a vulture from the bark. The bird, feeding on the carcases with which the earth was laden, did not return. Tezpi sent out other birds, of which the humming bird only came back, with a leafy branch in its beak. Then Tezpi, seeing that the country began to vegetate, left his bark on the mountain of Colhuacan."—Donelly's *Atlantis*, p. 99.

The tradition of a Deluge, "was the received notion under some form or other, of the most civilized people in the Old World, and of the barbarians of the New. The Aztecs combined with this some particular circumstances of a more arbitrary character, resembling the accounts of the east. They believed that two persons survived the Deluge, a man named Coxcox and his wife. Their heads are represented in ancient painting, together with a boat floating on the waters at the foot of a mountain. A dove is also depicted, with a hieroglyphical emblem of language in his mouth; which he is distributing to the children of Coxcox, who were born dumb. The neighboring people of Michoacan, inhabiting the same high plains of the Andes, had a still further tradition, that the boat in which Tegpi, their Noah, escaped, was filled with various kinds of animals and birds. After some time a vulture was sent out from it, but remained feeding on the dead bodies of the giants which had been left on the earth as the waters subsided. The little humming bird, *huitzitzilin*, was then sent forth, and returned with a twig in his mouth. The coincidence of both these accounts with the Hebrew and Chaldean narratives is obvious."—Prescott, *Conquest of Mexico*, pp. 463-4.

5. **Mexican Tradition Concerning the Savior**:—"The story of the life of the Mexican divinity, Quetzalcoatl, closely resembles that of the Savior; so closely, indeed, that we can come to no other conclusion than that Quetzalcoatl and Christ are the same being. But the history of the former has been handed down to us through an impure Lamanitish source, which has sadly disfigured and perverted the original incidents and teachings of the Savior's life and ministry. Regarding this god, Humboldt writes, 'How truly surprising is it to find that the Mexicans, who seem to have been unacquainted with the doctrine of the migration of the soul and the Metempsychosis *should have believed in the incarnation of the only Son of the supreme God, Tomacateuctli.* For Mexican mythology, speaking of no other Son of God except Quetzalcoatl, who was born of Chimelman, the virgin of Tula (without man), by His breath alone, by which may be signified His word or will, when it was announced to Chimelman, by the celestial messenger whom He despatched to inform her that she should conceive a son, it must be presumed this was Quetzalcoatl, who was the only son. Other authors might be adduced to show that the Mexicans believe that this Quetzalcoatl was both God and man; that He had, previously to His incarnation, existed from eternity, and that He had been the Creator both of the world and man; and that He had descended to reform the world by endurance, and being King of Tula, was crucified for the sins of mankind, etc., as is plainly declared in the tradition of Yucatan, and mysteriously represented in the Mexican paintings.'"—Pres. John Taylor, *Mediation and Atonement*, p. 201.

6. **Discoveries of Hebrew Inscriptions on Stone**:—"Between 1860 and 1865, four different stones with Hebrew inscriptions upon them were found in Licking County, Ohio, though not all in the same neighborhood. On one, which some suppose had been worn as an amulet, was a Hebrew inscription, which was translated, 'May the Lord have mercy on him a nephel;' that is, one of untimely birth. Elder Orson Pratt, however, was of the opinion that the final letter was a 't,'and that the legend should read,'May the Lord have mercy on him a Nephite.'

"Another of the stones bears a Hebrew inscription on each of its four sides. These inscriptions when translated read: 'The King of the Earth; The Law of the Lord: The Word of the Lord; The Holy of Holies.' It would be difficult to conceive that such an inscription would be put upon a stone by persons not acquainted with the law and with the word of the Lord; or who had not some idea regarding temple ordinances, and what the Holy of Holies implies. But a people like the Nephites would in all respects answer the requirements, as they were trained in both the law and the gospel."—Elder Geo. Reynolds, in his lecture, "*The Language of the Book of Mormon.*"

7. **Survival of the Hebrew Language among American Tribes**:—"It is claimed that such survivals are numerous in the religious songs and ceremonies of many of the tribes. A number of writers who visited or resided among the tribes of the northern continent, assert that the words Yehovah, Yah, Ale, and Hallelujah, could be distinctly heard in these exercises. Laet and Escarbotus assure us that they often heard the South American Indians repeat the sacred word Hallelujah."—Elder George Reynolds: "*The Language of the Book of Mormon.*"

Boudinot (see *Voice of Warning*, by Parley P. Pratt, 9th ed.) says concerning the language of the native American peoples:—"Their language, in its roots, idiom, and particular construction, appears to have the whole genius of the Hebrew; and, what is very remarkable and well worthy of serious attention, has most of the peculiarities of that language, especially those in which it differs from most other languages." Adair (*History of the American Indians*, London, 1775,) has written:—"The Indian language and dialects appear to have the very idiom and genius of the Hebrew. Their words and sentences are expressive, concise, emphatical, sonorous, and bold; and often, both in letters and significa- tion, synonymous with the Hebrew language."

8. **Tradition of an Ancient Record among the Natives of America:**—"It was well known to the Lamanites of this continent, at the time of the discovery of America by Europeans, that a book, such as is the Book of Mormon, existed among their remote ancestors; and that they themselves pos- sessed fragments of the record, though possibly in an altered form. The existence of these fragments was well known to the Spanish ecclesiastics who came to America; and, as they claimed to believe that the existence of such was a hindrance to the spread of Catholicism amongst the natives, they inflicted out- rageously cruel penalties upon any who attempted to conceal them. A very faint idea of what might have been published, had the Spaniards not pre- vented, may be surmised from the statement made by one author, that, 'They [the American aborigines] assert that a book was once in possession of their ancestors; and along with this recognition, they have traditions that the 'Great Spirit' used to foretell to their fathers future events; that he controlled nature in their favor; that angels once talked with them; that all the Indian tribes descended from one man who had twelve sons; that this man was a notable and renowned prince, having great dominions; and that the Indians, his posterity, will yet recover the same dominion and influence. They believe, by tradition, that the spirit of prophecy and miraculous interposition, once enjoyed by their ancestors, will yet be restored to them, and that they will recover the book, all of which has been so long lost.' [Colton,—*Origin of the American Indians*, London, 1833.] Could any one who has read the Book of Mormon give a better description of its contents than this extract does?" Reynolds,—*Language of the Book of Mormon.* Boudinot remarks of the Indians and their traditions:—"It is said among their principal or beloved men, that they have it handed down from their ancestors, that the book which the white people have was once theirs; that while they had it they prospered exceedingly," etc.

Boturini (p. 129) states that in Tula, about 660 A.D., "Huimatzin, a celebrated astronomer of the Toltecs, called together all the wise men, with the approval of the monarch, and painted that great book which they called Teoamoxtli, that is, 'divine book,' in which with distinct figures, account was given of the origin of the Indians; of the time of the separation of the people at the confusion of the language; of their peregrinations in Asia; of their first cities and towns that they had in America," etc., etc. We learn from the Book of Mormon, how that record,—itself the original sacred or "divine book" of the Lamanites,—was lost to them, inasmuch as the ancient plates were buried by Moroni about 420 A.D. The compilation of the "Teoamoxtli" or divine book of the Toltecs, was probably an attempt to recover through tradition and such fragmental records as existed, those ancient scriptures.—(See article by Moses Thatcher, *Contributor*, ii, 223-224.)

N. B.—The items presented on this page are additional to the "Notes" which are appended to the "Book of Mormon" lectures as published in the "Articles of Faith."